FRANCES CASHEL HOEY
1830-1908

A BIBLIOGRAPHY

compiled by

P.D. Edwards

Victorian Fiction Research Guides VIII

Department of English

University of Queensland

ISBN 0 86776 083 4

ISSN 015 3921

Published by
Department of English
University of Queensland
St Lucia
Australia 4067

VICTORIAN FICTION RESEARCH GUIDES

Victorian Fiction Research Guides are issued by the Victorian Fiction Group within the Department of English, University of Queensland.

The group concentrates on minor or lesser known writers active during the period from about 1860 to about 1910. Among the writers we are presently working on are Victoria Cross, Mary and Jane Helen Findlater, Annie Hector, Annie Thomas, Morley Roberts, E.L. Voynich, Mary Linskill, Eliza Lynn Linton, Ethel M. Dell, Beatrice Harraden, Mrs Campbell Praed, and Rosa N. Carey. Journals being indexed include *Belgravia*, *The Woman at Home*, and *Pall Mall Magazine*.

We should be interested to hear from anyone else working on any of these writers or journals, and any information about the location of manuscript and other material would be most welcome. Since there will inevitably be gaps and errors in our published bibliographies, we should also be grateful for information about these.

The subscription for the second series of Victorian Fiction Research Guides (V - VIII) is $20 (Australian). Individual volumes cost $5. Copies of the first series (I - IV) are available at $16 for the whole series or $5 for individual titles.

Orders should be sent to Mrs Barbara Garlick, Division of External Studies, and correspondence on other matters to Professor P.D. Edwards, Department of English, University of Queensland, St Lucia, Australia 4067.

The Victorian Fiction Group acknowledges generous financial support from the Australian Research Grants Committee, the University of Queensland Research Committee, and the Department of English, University of Queensland.

i

CONTENTS

INTRODUCTION

In the 1870s and 1880s Frances Cashel Hoey briefly won a reputation as a novelist a little cleverer and more serious than the general run. During the same period, and for a decade longer, her many translations from the French helped to keep her name before the public. A select few would also have known her as one of the most prolific reviewers in the *Spectator*. For a short time, in the early 1870s, she even achieved a degree of notoriety - though again within a limited circle - as supposed collaborator on a number of novels purporting to be the unaided work of Edmund Yates. But chiefly her life and literary endeavours are a saga of unremitting struggle meagrely rewarded, either by fame or by fortune. The last twenty years of her life were spent in obscurity and what she felt to be undeserved neglect. Her financial position, precarious even during her most creative period, when she also had her husband's earnings to supplement her own, seems to have been always more or less desperate during the sixteen years of her widowhood. The only new editions of her novels were pirated (or so she believed); those of which she still owned the copyright, or could purchase it with her last ten pounds, were never given the chance of attracting the new generation of readers that she hoped for. Though unmistakably a lady of intelligence, vivacity, and resourcefulness, she toiled all her life in depressing proximity to New Grub Street.

One of Mrs Hoey's proudest memories in old age
was of having been introduced, as a young married
girl, to the great Daniel O'Connell.[1] The meeting
must have taken place in 1846 or early 1847, just
before O'Connell's death. Frances Sarah Johnston,
born near Dublin on 15 February 1830,[2] had married
Adam Murray Stewart on her sixteenth birthday, and
throughout her life up till then O'Connell ('the
Liberator') had been uncrowned king of Ireland.
Members of her own family had been active in the
uprising of 1798, and when she began her literary
career, in 1853, it was as a contributor to two
journals closely identified with Irish nationalism,
the *Freeman's Journal* and the *Nation*. Most of her
associates at this time had been members of Young
Ireland, which had led an ineffectual rebellion
against British rule in 1848. One of them, William
Carleton, gave her introductions to Thackeray and
the editor of the *Morning Post* when she went to
London just after the death of her husband in
November 1855. Another, Charles Gavan Duffy, had
been one of the founders of the *Nation* and was
its editor when Frances Stewart began writing for
it; later, after emigrating to Australia and
becoming Premier of Victoria, he was to provide John
Cashel Hoey with a job, as secretary to the colony's
Agent-General in London, which appears to have been
his main source of income for fifteen of the last
twenty years of his life. Cashel Hoey, assistant
editor of the *Nation* from 1849 to 1855 and editor
in 1856 and 1857, became Frances's second husband on
6 February 1858.

According to the *DNB*, Frances Johnston's father
was   secretary and registrar to the Mount Jermone
cemetry in Dublin and his daughter, one of eight
children, was largely self-educated. Her mother had
been a Shaw, half-sister of Bernard Shaw's mother, and
if money was as short in the Johnston household as in
that of the Shaws, Frances's parents may have
welcomed her early marriage to Adam Murray Stewart

2

(though on the evidence of her novels Frances would
never have married but for love - and for
imperishable first love). The fact that she took
to journalism within seven years of her marriage,
at a time when she had two daughters to look after,
may indicate that her circumstances remained
difficult and that the illness, if illness it was,
that carried Stewart off two years later had
already incapacitated him. At any rate her
decision, immediately after his death, to pursue a
literary career in London was presumably governed
by the necessity of earning a living as well as by
thirst for literary glory.

In the event, however, it seems to have taken
her many years to gain even a toehold in the London
literary world. The *DNB* states that in her first
two years there, before her second marriage early
in 1858, she wrote reviews for the *Morning Post* and
the *Spectator*, but it is unlikely that her
connexion with the *Spectator* began before 1861,
when Richard Holt Hutton, a close friend of her
second husband, became editor. Cashel Hoey moved
to London a few months after his marriage, having
sold his interest in the *Nation*, of which he was by
then editor and part-owner. Three years later he
was called to the bar of the Middle Temple, but
journalism probably remained his chief occupation -
as well as his wife's - for at least the next ten
years. In 1865 he became assistant to the editor
of the *Dublin Review*, W.G. Ward, a position he
remained in till 1879, and both he and Frances
became occasional contributors to the *Review*.
Though apparently living in London from the time of
their marriage, they do not appear to have acquired
any permanent home there until 1868, when they
moved to 17 Campden Hill Road, Kensington: this
remained their residence until John Cashel Hoey's
death in 1892.[3]

Neither Mrs Hoey's reminiscences in her letters
to Edmund Downey (the richest store of information

about her life), nor other people's observations of
her, throw much light on her literary activities
and style of life in the 1850s and 1860s. At the
time of Oscar Wilde's death in 1900, she recalled
having held the 'dreadful wretch' in her arms just
after he was born; later, she said, he had been a
playmate, though much younger, of her own children:[4]
as Wilde was not born till October 1854, however,
this would have been possible only if the children
remained in Dublin when Frances went to live in
London at the beginning of 1856. Presumably it was
soon after (or even before) her second marriage that
she, and perhaps her husband, began making the long
and frequent visits to France that continued, for
her, until only a few years before her death.[5] As
far as I know there is no way of ascertaining what
kind of material she contributed to the *Morning Post*
and during what period, and none of her
contributions to the *Spectator* - whenever they began
- can be identified before the 1870s. She may have
found other outlets for her literary efforts in the
early 1860s, but the first contribution to a journal
that can be identified definitely as her work was
the sensational novella *Buried in the Deep*,
serialized in *Chambers's Magazine* in February 1865.
Over the next ten years (not, however, the next
thirty as the *DNB* asserts) *Chambers's* published
several more stories, two novels, and many reviews
by her. In the second half of the sixties she also
began contributing to *Temple Bar*, then edited by
Edmund Yates, and her work continued to appear
there, infrequently, until the late seventies. Her
first published novel, *A House of Cards* (1868), was
serialized in *Tinsley's Magazine*, of which Yates
became founding editor after leaving *Temple Bar*.

A *House of Cards* is a fairly routine,
nondescript sensation story, heavily emphasizing
such stock themes as the irrestible power of
retributive fate, the ineluctability of hereditary
evil, and the delusoriness of man's (or more
specifically, woman's) belief that early misdeeds

or mistakes can be permanently lived down and concealed. Slapdash in both style and structure, the novel gives the impression of having been made to order, perhaps specifically to the editorial order of Yates, whose own novels provide some of the most obvious models for the female character, haunted by her past and by her unwanted son, who is the main centre of consciousness. As a woman Mrs Hoey perhaps evinces a little more sympathy for her peccant heroine than Yates is able to muster for, say, Margaret Dacre in his *Land at Last*; there is also an individual, and essentially feminine, touch in the sensitive psychological study of the heroine's blind mother-in-law; and at least one of Mrs Hoey's most characteristic topics, the power of impending death to concentrate the human mind on the eternal verities of religion, receives its first expression as the villain's innocent young wife prepares herself for a violent death at his hands. But on the whole *A House of Cards* is undistinguished even for a first novel, and unusually silly, particularly in its 'pagan' fatalism,[6] even for a sensation novel of the 1860s.

The reminders of Edmund Yates in *A House of Cards*, though strong, can be adequately accounted for by his editorial influence and by the 'house-style' of Tinsley Brothers, proprietors of the magazine in which the novel was serialized and publishers of it in book-form. Many years later, however, William Tinsley was to publish a series of allegations that may appear to provide a further and altogether more cogent explanation - one that would lead us, indeed, to expect far stronger traces of Yates in her first novel. Tinsley alleged that Mrs Hoey was actually the unacknowledged author of large parts of four Yates novels and of another in its entirety; and all four of the novels of which he credited her with part-authorship - *Land at Last* (1866), *A Forlorn Hope* (1867), *Black Sheep* (1867), and *The Rock*

Ahead (1868) - were written shortly before *A House of Cards* began its serialization.

Tinsley's story and the evidence for and against it are discussed at length in the introduction to my bibliography of Edmund Yates (Victorian Fiction Research Guides, III, 1980, pp. 27-34). The story, first published in print in Tinsley's *Random Recollections of an Old Publisher* (1900), was accepted as true by Elizabeth Lee, author of the article on Mrs Hoey in the *DNB*; but it was subsequently denied by Yates's son Edmund Smedley Yates and, on three separate occasions, by T.H.S. Escott, a friend of both Yates and Mrs Hoey who asserted that he had heard both of them pronounce it untrue.[7] Escott maintained, on the basis of what they had told him, that their collaboration had extended no further than Yates's having discussed some of his ideas, and sometimes his actual drafts, with Mrs Hoey, whose comments and suggested revisions had usually been made 'conversationally' but had occasionally been put in writing as well. Tinsley's allegation, on this flimsy basis, that Yates and Mrs Hoey had conspired to defraud him by passing off Mrs Hoey's work as Yates's - at twice the price that Mrs Hoey would have been able to command under her own name - was castigated by Escott as 'pure fable'.

At the time when I wrote the introduction to my bibliography of Yates I concluded that on the available evidence it was impossible to decide which, if either, was the true version of the collaboration, Tinsley's or Escott's. I noted that Tinsley, on his own admission and probably with good reason, bore Yates a grudge. I also pointed to the difficulty of reconciling his assertion that Mrs Hoey herself betrayed the conspiracy (because she felt Yates had treated her badly) with the fact that they remained friends until her death. And with regard to Tinsley's most crucial piece of evidence - the fact, or alleged fact, that the manuscript of *A Righted Wrong* was wholly in Mrs Hoey's handwriting and that of the other four novels partly in hers and partly in Yates's - I pointed out that verification is impossible in the absence of the manuscripts themselves: while Tinsley himself undoubtedly had access to them, there appears to be no record of his having shown them to any independent witness. At that stage I had not found any statements by other people to corroborate Tinsley's charges; but neither had I found any denials, apart from Escott's.

Since then, however, I have read Mrs Hoey's correspondence with Edmund Downey, which includes several allusions to the alleged collaboration. Though somewhat cryptic and confusing, these tend to support Tinsley's account rather than Escott's - but with one important difference.

Mrs Hoey's allusions to the matter were prompted by three separate events: the death and funeral of Yates in May 1894, the publication of Tinsley's *Random Recollections* in September 1900, and the publication of Downey's *Twenty Years Ago; a Book of Anecdote, Illustrating Literary Life in London* in February 1905. Mrs Hoey told Downey that she had had a 'long interview' with Yates on the Tuesday before his death (which occurred on Sunday, 20 May 1894). The death had shocked her profoundly, particularly as she was to have dined with him and Mrs Yates at the Oatlands Hotel on the very day of the funeral service - 'a chapter in the tragi-comedy of life which it is *quite impossible* that anybody there *could have* read as I read it, for reasons.' At the service (on 24 May 1894) she saw Tinsley, obviously for the first time in many years. Tinsley by this time had suffered several bankruptcies and was known to be addicted to the bottle. 'Poor old Tinsley!' she exclaims, in a postscript to the letter from which I have just quoted. 'I am so sorry for him. We looked at each other, coming out of the [Savoy] Chapel, and each knew exactly what was in the mind of the other. How badly he was treated by everybody in that clever, unprincipled set, and still worse, I am afraid, by himself.'[8] The two passages offer a good sample of the romancing, the delight in mystification which continued to colour Mrs Hoey's references to the portentous subject. Tantalizingly, and it seems reluctantly, she remained big with her secret for the rest of her life.

The appearance of Tinsley's *Recollections* in 1900 at first made her 'nervous and unhappy about the Yates business'[9] and subsequently caused her 'annoyance' which she was sure Tinsley himself would have regretted.[10] Friends and relatives wrote to her asking her whether she had been '"blackmailed" in the matter'.[11] A 'certain publisher' asserted to one of her friends that she 'had taken the credit of Mr. Y's novels, not he of mine', and this 'pretty version' of the story had gained currency in America, perhaps as a result of the efforts of an American whom she had previously reported as having 'got on the trail of the EY affair': he may have been the Mr A.M. Bradley who later tried to 'open up communications with me, which I am sure meant the Tinsley business'.[12] So many lies and false conjectures were circulating that she was tempted to tell the true story and to tell it all. She had resolved to do so, 'if there is another chance', as early as February 1901, in response to the *canard* that she rather than Yates was laying false claim to the authorship of the novels. In an undated letter probably written in the second half of 1902 she hinted that she might be willing to write the story for *T.P.'s Weekly*, of which Downey was then editor and for which she was convinced it would make 'a grand *coup* of ex-post facto literary gossip'.

Apparently Downey failed to respond to the suggestion; nor did he avail himself of the opportunity to comment on the matter in his memoirs, *Twenty Years Ago*, published in 1905 - though the book was dedicated to Mrs Hoey and actually quoted in full (but without naming her as the author) the passage from her letter to him in which she reported her meeting with Tinsley at Yates's funeral and lamented the bad treatment he had received from 'that clever unprincipled set'.[13] Removed from its context, the passage throws no light at all on the composition of the 'set' who so mistreated Tinsley. Thanking Downey for her copy of the book, Mrs Hoey said nothing about the quotation from her letter but complained at the omission of *A House of Cards* from Downey's list of promising first novels which appeared in *Tinsley's Magazine*; almost in the same breath, however, she shifted to the matter that presumably had been really on her mind all along: 'I wish the Yates business might turn up again. (When we meet you shall know why) it would be better it should - but this is strictly for *you only*.'[14] The momentousness of her promised disclosures is marked by the regal italics (which recall those she had used earlier when commenting on the 'tragi-comedy' by which her planned last dinner with Yates had turned out to be his funeral).

Three and a half years after the appearance of Downey's memoirs Mrs Hoey herself was dead, and I have found no indication that she did succeed in making the Yates business turn up again in the meantime. Perhaps Downey, when he heard what she wanted to say and why, may have persuaded her that even the fullest and most sympathetic account of the affair would not be certain to redound to her credit and that she would, in any case, gain scant kudos from having helped write a handful of novels by now forgotten, or at best 'half-forgotten' - like

Black Sheep which had reappeared, in the series Half-Forgotten Novels, in 1904.[15]

Mrs Hoey's references to the affair implicitly confirm all but one of Tinsley's assertions. They make it clear that she did regard herself as author or joint-author of some of Yates's novels, presumably the ones that Tinsley named. They also lend a decided air of probability to Tinsley's statement that Mrs Hoey herself had let out the secret of the surreptitious collaboration, presumably because she had felt she was not receiving proper credit or payment for her work. The one important particular that Mrs Hoey apparently rejects in Tinsley's version of the story is his insistence that he knew nothing about the collaboration until Mrs Hoey told him, that he was in fact a victim rather than an agent of the conspiracy to pass off inferior literary wares as a first-class and recognized product. Mrs Hoey's rejoinder to this is emphatic but not unequivocal: 'Tinsley never *was* deceived - no one wanted to deceive him - he had [?*bales*] of my copy.'[16] Here, in her only comment on this aspect of the matter, Mrs Hoey may be saying either that Tinsley knew all along of the collaboration between Yates and herself, or that she (and perhaps Yates) *assumed* that he knew, or simply that he *should* have known (and perhaps that it was his own fault if he didn't). Tinsley had accused her of having been a party to a fraud, against him and against the public. Understandably, but not altogether convincingly, she denies any fraud, or at least any awareness of fraud, against Tinsley on her part; and as for fraud against the public she would no doubt have argued that the novels produced jointly by her and Yates, or by her on her own, were of just as good quality as Yates's independent creations, and that one of them, *Black Sheep*, was probably the most popular and most highly regarded of 'Yates's' novels. Both she and Tinsley tell the story in such a way as to exculpate themselves, she of having, as an author, defrauded her publisher; he of having, as a publisher, defrauded his public. Unless new facts come to light the truth of the matter must remain uncertain: neither Mrs Hoey's nor Tinsley's version rings altogether true,[17] and Escott's very different version still cannot be ruled out of court.

A minor mystery connected with the publication of Tinsley's *Recollections* is the whereabouts of a letter or review by Yates's son, Edmund Smedley Yates, evidently defending his father against Tinsley's aspersions. Smedley's communication on the matter is referred to cryptically by Mrs Hoey in her letter to Downey of 13 November [?1900]: 'I wonder no one has observed that E.S.Y. gave himself away by using the word "Hush-money" - Mrs [?Horne] Payne saw it at once.' I have been unable to find any published letter or review by Smedley Yates at this time, and there is no reference to any in his scrapbook - to which I have recently gained access. There is no mention of Tinsley's book in the *World*, of which Smedley Yates was still co-proprietor. Perhaps his comments were made in a private letter - to Mrs Hoey herself or to a mutual friend - which had been seen by Downey, by Mrs [?Horne] Payne, and presumably by other members of Mrs Hoey's circle. Alternatively, they may have been published in one of the provincial newspapers for which, at various times, Smedley Yates worked as a journalist. It is even conceivable, if Mrs Hoey's letter offers a fair sample of their contents, that they were published in an American paper, to circumvent English libel laws: this might account for the special interest taken in the matter in America and the annoying importunities of the American newshound, A.M. Bradley, which Mrs Hoey remarks upon in some of her letters to Downey. Certainly, unless he had incontrovertible proof, English libel laws would have made it dangerous for

Smedley Yates to accuse Tinsley or Mrs Hoey of
accepting 'hush-money' from his father.

An amusingly garbled account of the story of
the alleged collaboration is given by Harry
Furniss in his book *Some Victorian Women* (1923):

> I recollect a rather pretty little woman
> I used to meet at Tinsley's, the
> publisher. She wrote for him, but she
> also wrote other novels, that she
> declared - and Tinsley assured me he
> knew her statement to be true - she
> sold to Edmund Yates, who published them
> as his own productions. When she died I
> read with much interest the obituary
> notice of her written by Yates, which I,
> reading between the lines, was fully
> convinced confirmed the strange
> statement she herself had made. Anyway
> he never published another novel . . . .[18]

In the absence of any other published descriptions
of Mrs Hoey, it would be gratifying to be able to
accept Furniss's testimony that she was, in her
forties, 'a rather pretty little woman'; but
nearly everything else in the passage is so wrong
as to strip him of every shred of credibility.
Yates in fact died fourteen years before Mrs Hoey
and certainly didn't compose her obituary before
doing so; and far from deserting fiction after his
alleged collaboration with her finished, he went
on to publish at least nine more novels. Faulty
as his memory was, however, it is hard to believe
that Furniss can simply have imagined meeting Mrs
Hoey and hearing her speak of the collaboration.

Whatever the truth of the matter, the nature
and extent of Mrs Hoey's contribution to novels
published under Yates's name between 1866 and
1870 are too problematic to make it safe to
include the novels, or any parts of them, among
her works. *A Righted Wrong* (1870), which she

was alleged to have written on her own, certainly
reads more like a woman's, and specifically a Hoey
novel than most of Yates's other novels; but on
internal evidence it is hard to believe that she
can have been responsible for more than small parts
of most of the others: in particular, it seems
practically inconceivable that Yates himself was
not responsible for nearly all of *Black Sheep*,
though Mrs Hoey could have had a larger hand in *A
Forlorn Hope*.

Mrs Hoey's remaining ten novels, published
during the next twenty years, at gradually
lengthening intervals, all conform essentially to
the pattern established in her first. Her plots
continue to unfold bewilderingly intricate webs of
relationship among groups of characters seemingly
worlds apart from each other - often divided
literally by oceans, as well as by circumstance.
The coincidences, whether interpreted as
manifestations of providence, fate, romance, or
mere accident, become if possible even more
marvellous and unpredictable. Weakness and shabby
villainy constantly expose virtue, female virtue
especially, to pain and moral danger; and deep in
the shadows lurk vicious criminals whose blows or
revelations produce unexpectedly lurid climaxes to
otherwise quite tame third volumes. Heredity is
always a major determinant of characters' vices,
and sometimes of their more agreeable talents,
and in the age-old tradition of romance inherited
qualities frequently signal a character's true
identity to the reader long before it is formally
disclosed. Mistakes of identity, resulting
particularly from impersonation or the existence
of 'doubles', are a common source of plot
complications. Death, by natural or unnatural
means, can always be relied on to remove
inconvenient characters, the vicious and the
virtuous alike. In her choice of plot materials,
Mrs Hoey never outgrew the influence of Dickens,
Wilkie Collins, and the sensational potboilers

of the 1860s. Mystery and violence, the macabre
and the exotic were the lifeblood of her romantic
imagination - the same imagination as compelled
her, in real life, to make such a tantalizing
mystery of her collaboration with Yates, or to
invest a sudden journey she made to Paris at the
time of the Commune with all the mysterious danger
and urgency of an episode from *A Tale of Two
Cities*.[19]

Despite their preposterous, and often clumsily
managed plots, however, the novels are by no means
devoid of wit and moral sense. In their treatment
of love especially, they ring some surprising and
refreshing changes on the conventions of Victorian
romance. Though the characters and situations can
usually be fitted more or less neatly into the
familiar moulds of sentimental fiction (a fact
which Mrs Hoey underlines by constantly invoking
parallels in the novels of Jane Austen or Dickens,
Trollope or Thackeray), the outcomes of the love
stories, the distribution of rewards and
punishments, and the assessment of what really
constitutes a reward and what a punishment for a
given pair of lovers often imply a subtle, serious,
and unexpected disavowal of sentimental norms.
Ostensibly, Mrs Hoey's own attitudes to love could
hardly be more conventional or more conservative.
First love is nearly always ineffacable. True
lovers are always unselfish and disinterested.
Even the strongest and truest love must be
subordinated to duty and self-respect. A true
lover remains faithful even when his love is
thwarted by circumstance or betrayed by the
beloved. Unlike many other popular sentimental
novelists, however, Mrs Hoey was well aware that
in the real world such absolutism in love (or *of*
love) not only militated against a smooth path for
true lovers but was also as likely as not to leave
them still unsatisfied at the end of the path.
False love, on the other hand, or true love
compromised, can be better at clearing the

obstacles in its path and at bearing its final disappointments, because it is often suppler, more resilient.

The contrasting fates of the two heroines of *A Golden Sorrow* (1872) provide the first and one of the best examples of this reversal of conventional expectations. Florence Reeve, one of Mrs Hoey's 'angelic' heroines, marries for love, endures poverty and separation from her husband with patience and fortitude, wears the disguise and performs the duties of a mere maid without any loss of dignity, remains ever sweet, charitable, and self-effacing even when nursing her ogrish father-in-law through his terminal illness, receives, miraculously, his deathbed blessing when she confesses her true identity, and at the peak of her material fortunes finds that even before this he had made a will leaving her almost the whole of his estate as a reward for her nursing. Miriam Clint, her husband's sister, looks at her best on horseback (usually a bad sign in novels of the 1860s and 1870s), boldly embarks on a mercenary marriage to an old man in order to escape from the household of her appalling father, and suffers the approved punishment when her husband turns out to be mean, jealous, tyrannical, and (it is strongly hinted) brutal in bed - a replica in almost all respects of the father whom he had replaced as her master. Yet at the end of the novel Miriam, the 'childless wife', 'the woman who has never loved', is rewarded with a husband whom she loves and who loves her, even though by this time she has added to her crimes by inducing her brother to impersonate her recently dead husband and fabricate a will leaving the husband's estate to her. Florence, a 'true woman, who incapable of the moral discord implied in deserting her own sphere, assiduously aspires to the best standard of duty and culture within it', receives no more tangible reward than another man to nurse, this time her husband, whose baby she had borne and

lost in its infancy, from whom she has been
uncomplainingly separated ever since, and who
finally returns to her (from the Californian
goldfields) stricken with a fever that produces
amnesia, diminished responsibility, and eventually
a state of languid imbecility! It appears that
Miriam will not be blessed with children, but
otherwise her happiness promises to be unclouded
except by the plight of her brother and her angelic
sister-in-law.

As epigraph to *A Golden Sorrow*, Mrs Hoey uses
Shakespeare's lines, ''tis better to be lowly born,/
And range with humble livers in content,/Than to be
perked up in a glistering grief,/And wear a golden
sorrow'. But although the pursuit of gold brings
bitter sorrow to Miriam's brother and for a time to
Miriam herself, the alternative rewards allotted to
Florence, the lowly born humble-liver, are hardly
calculated to recommend themselves to the ordinary
reader of sentimental love stories. At first
glance, indeed, the novel's message may appear
obscure and probably confused. Reading Mrs Hoey's
other novels, however, one comes to recognize how
radically her conception of a 'happy ending' can
differ from that which her romantic plot-materials
and her conventional attitudes to love may seem to
predicate. Absolute as the lover's, and the
reader's, imagination may believe it, the
happiness to be found in the fulfilment of human
love often turns out disappointing and delusory,
and in at least one later novel the heroine ends
by stigmatizing her unswerving fidelity to an
earthly lover as a form of 'idolatry',
deflecting her from the only true object of
worship. Miriam earns her happy ending, after
all her sins, not only by an oddly incomplete act
of secular reparation - renouncing all but £5000
of her husband's estate - but also, and more
significantly, by transcending merely secular
morality, by learning to mourn, after 'many
sleepless nights' and 'long days of perplexity and

softening', not because her 'sin had "found her out"' but because 'she had "done this great wickedness *against God*"' (Mrs Hoey's italics). For a shallow nature like Miriam's, this represents a great step upwards, almost comparable to the miraculous deathbed redemption of her father-in-law. (It makes an interesting contrast to the purely secular repentance, dictated largely by love, of Trollope's Lady Ongar, who similarly renounced the fortune she had won by a mercenary marriage but also hung on to enough to keep her comfortable.[20]) Florence, however, like most of Mrs Hoey's true heroines, understands instinctively that all human aspirations, including love, must be compounded with love and service to God if they are to escape the taint of selfishness, if they are to give adequate expression to the nobler (Godlike) attributes of human nature.

One of Mrs Hoey's later novels, *The Lover's Creed* (1884), takes its title from the sentimental dictum, 'One, and one only, is the Lover's Creed', but this is a tale in which the heroine, Mavis Reeve (who 'looks like a saint, and sings like an angel'), and the deserving hero are kept apart simply by a prolonged sequence of accidents, not by any conflicting ties or duties. Like Madeleine Kindersley in *Griffith's Double* (1876), perhaps the most idealized and morally impressive of all Mrs Hoey's heroines, the heroine of *The Lover's Creed* lives and loves so sacramentally that Providence appears almost demonstrably her sole guide. Even so, Mavis is vouchsafed the opportunity for a Christlike sacrifice, using herself as decoy for an assassin's knife that was intended for her pupil (Mavis is Mrs Hoey's only governess-heroine). In contrast, heroines like Florence, or like the innocently bigamous wife in *Falsely True*, are given their brief interval of happiness in love *before* being called upon for their great sacrifice - presumably, for both of them a lifelong sacrifice. The difference appears to be explained chiefly by the faults of the men to whom they give their hearts, faults which Mrs Hoey, obliquely defending her heroines' taste, is at pains to put down (in Trollopian fashion) to weakness and shabbiness rather than outright evil, even though in one case they lead to bigamy and in the other to forgery. There is no suggestion, however, that the sacrifices and loss of happiness that are visited upon the heroines are to be viewed as a punishment or an expiation; on the contrary, in forgiving and, for as long as possible, serving the men who have wronged them they evidently achieve a reward beside which mere sensual gratification pales.

Another heroine who loves a personable man not quite worthy of her, Janet Monro in *All, or Nothing* (1879), receives a double reward: saving her beloved husband from a would-be assassin and expiring immediately afterwards from the shock. Already, upon realizing that her husband did not love her as she loved him and was in a state of 'profound ennui', she had learnt 'the ordinary lesson of human experience, that the worship of a human being is idolatry', and her dying words are 'Thou shalt have no other gods but Me'; but the novel leaves no doubt that death has no sting for her. Laura, the girl her husband had loved first and always, reflects after Janet's death that Janet had been 'worth a million of me' and her own husband Robert Thornton 'worth a million of Edward Dunstan', her lover; 'yet they are gone, and we are left'. She asks, 'Why? Ah me! why?' and Mrs Hoey responds: '. . . it did not come to Laura's mind that perhaps just that difference of value may have furnished the why.'

Though I have stressed the religious element in Mrs Hoey's love stories, I do not wish to give the impression that she is recognizably a religious novelist, or that she wears her piety on her sleeve like such writers as Charlotte M. Yonge, Elizabeth Sewell, or even Mrs Craik. Rather the reverse. The religious beliefs that inform her treatment of

love in many of her novels are generally voiced so
quietly and discreetly that they can be overlooked,
leaving the reader with the impression of nothing but
a rather capricious manipulation of the secular
morality of the conventional love story. As a Roman
Catholic - born a Protestant but converted at the
time of her second marriage - Mrs Hoey certainly
wished to propagate her faith. She played an active
part in Catholic charities (as well as in such
secular 'good causes' as the Anti-Vivisection League
and the Society for Sick Children); she wrote at
least one devotional book (*Nazareth*, 1873); and her
private correspondence is full of religious
sentiments which never sound merely perfunctory. But
in her novels she generally avoids advocating
specifically Catholic views. One exception is *Out of
Court* (1874), which has as its central theme the evil
and sacrilege of secular divorce and which openly
applauds Ireland for rejecting the institution:
opposition to divorce, however, was not confined to
Catholics, and most reviewers seem to have seen
nothing offensively sectarian in Mrs Hoey's raising
of the subject, nor in the fact that one of the
characters who are most outspoken about it is a
Protestant whose conversion to Catholicism, when she
finds that her 'human love and human wisdom' avail
nothing without 'the Love that is Divine, and the
wisom that is unerring', is foreshadowed throughout
the novel. Later, in *The Question of Cain* (1882),
the villain begins thinking about religion after a
conversation with a Roman Catholic priest and,
under this providential influence, repeats the
Lord's Prayer to himself just before being bloodily
murdered (in the sensational climax to the most
sensational of Mrs Hoey's novels); it also appears
that the heroine of the novel may marry one of the
priest's parishioners. And in *The Lover's Creed*
the hero is a Catholic and the heroine, Mavis
Quinn, already 'struck with great amazement' after
attending a Catholic church for a while, is
'received into the church' on her supposed death

bed - from which she subsequently recovers. Generally
however, Mrs Hoey seems to have wished her novels to
look little different from the kind of secular
sentimental romance that one of the characters in *The
Lover's Creed*, a woman of forty, writes under the
pseudonym of 'Ignota':

> In her hand was the wand of a magician; it
> conferred or withheld the heart's desire of
> those whom the wielder of it summoned up
> from phantasmal realms . . . . She could
> summon up beautiful images of girlhood, set
> them in her pages, crown them with glory and
> honour, enrich them with love, fortune,
> happiness; or she could gently withdraw them
> from a world that did not appreciate, or
> might fail to satisfy them, by that
> beneficent expedient of early and poetical
> death which was not absolutely forbidden to
> the novelist thirty years ago. Psychology
> and physiology did not hold their terrors
> over the story-tellers of those days.

In the heyday of Zola (whom she detested) Mrs Hoey
was well aware that her kind of novel appeared old
hat.

A few other aspects of her fiction are worth
brief mention.

For all her connexions with Irish nationalism
in the 1840s and 1850s, she never attempted to
identify herself as an Irish novelist. Presumably,
like Trollope, she recognized that by the 1860s
'Irish subjects generally [had] become distasteful
to English readers'.[21] She must also have known
that no English publisher or editor would willingly
have provided her with an outlet for the intense
nationalism and radically anti-British, anti-
imperialist feeling that flashes up repeatedly in
her letters to her compatriot Edmund Downey. Irish
characters figure in a number of the novels, but

they are as often weak and disreputable as morally admirable. Irish settings are used extensively only in *Out of Court* and in three novellas - *The Queen's Token* (1875), *No Sign* (1875), and *Ralph Craven's Silver Whistle* (1877) - of which two are historical romances. There is warm praise for the distinctive Irish beauty of one of the women in *Falsely True*, but nothing but scorn for the other Irish woman who appears in the same novel, a 'sordid, grovelling, selfish' actress who is compared to Becky Sharp. In *Out of Court* the 'intonation' of the Irish gentry is carefully distinguished from the 'brogue' with which it is sometimes 'confounded', even by writers who know Ireland, and the Irish peasantry are represented as possessing 'neither the brutal density of the English, nor the cold, suspicious, self-sufficing reserve of the Scottish lower orders, wherewith to disgust, repel, and mortify'. The bigamous Irish hero of *Falsely True*, though a 'dreamer' and graceful almost to the point of prettiness and effeminacy, at least has the knack of 'getting on' with foreigners which the English, being 'less adaptive and tolerant', lack. English insolence towards foreigners, and particularly towards subject races, also comes in for acidulous criticism from time to time: in *The Question of Cain*, for example, the response of a Parisian concierge to the haughtiness and insularity of English visitors is eloquently rendered, and in *The Blossoming of an Aloe* (1875) the 'cruelties' of the British in India after the Mutiny, and the 'fine Britannic insolence' which cannot believe that a 'slight knowledge of [India] and the history of its people' might benefit its rulers, are roundly condemned. As a journalist, however, Mrs Hoey carefully avoids offending English sensitivities even when reporting such an event as Edward VII's visit to Dublin in 1903;[22] whereas her private correspondence, around the same time, bristles with bitter denunciations of British policy in Ireland (particularly under Balfour), British atrocities in China and South Africa (the latter under the command of the renegade Irishman

Kitchener), and British foreign policy's fatuous
jealousy and distrust of France. In her novels,
too, her Irishness is so muted that when T.P.
O'Connor was compiling his *Cabinet of Irish
Literature*, consisting of biographies of and
extracts from contemporary Irish writers, he had to
ask her husband, who had already been chosen for
inclusion, whether she also was Irish: O'Connor's
impression was that she was not.[23] No such doubt
could have existed about the nationality of her
cousin Bernard Shaw!

Except in relation to Ireland, Mrs Hoey's
political, social, and moral attitudes appear to
have been generally conservative. As a lifelong
Francophile and student of French history, however,
she was able to withstand a firsthand experience of
the Paris Commune without the frenzies of horror it
aroused in so many English people; and while her
novels and journalism contain denunciations of
trends in modern life that she finds disagreeable -
the Aesthetic and women's rights movements, the
decline of feminine modesty, the shiftless langour
of modern young men, the growing tolerance of
marital infidelity in London society, the filth of
Zolaism - she can also speak feelingly, and with
unexpected cynicism, about the ancient wrongs of
women, the fickleness of men's love, and the
silliness of many of the restraints women were
expected to impose on their emotions. For example,
in the novel aptly called *The Lover's Creed*, a
lyrical proposal-scene, enacted in 'the good old
style' as Mrs Hoey approvingly notes, is followed
by a little dialogue in which the triumphant hero,
who must leave immediately for the war, concedes
that the separation may be worse for the woman he
leaves behind than for himself and adds, with
apparently gratuitous bitterness, 'They always say
so; they do that much justice to women, at all
costs'. To which Mrs Hoey appends her own caustic
comment: 'It is surprising what broad views of
the virtues and sufferings of the whole female sex

a man will take when he is in love; it is equally
remarkable how his vision contracts when he has got
out of love.' Coming as it does after a model
proposal from an obviously sincere young man, the
comment must raise questions in the reader's mind
about Mrs Hoey's own experiences of love and
marriage and the, for the most part hidden,
intensity of her feminist feelings. Perhaps her
first, shortlived marriage turned out badly, and
even her second, though she always professed the
profoundest love and respect for her husband before
and after his death, may have had serious drawbacks:
however loving he may or may not have remained, the
evidence of his wife's chronic shortage of money
suggests that he may have been a rather poor
provider, not always given to sharing his worldly
goods with her.

Mrs Hoey's novels throw a clearer light on
some other aspects of her life and character.
These include her love of theatre - which emerges
both explicitly and implicitly in the novels and is
confirmed in the 'Lady's Letter' which she
contributed to the *Australasian* for many years - and
her interest, in her later years at least, in
psychic phenomena: this found expression in her
lively and sympathetic portrayal of a 'modern'
young lady with apparently psychic powers, Amabel
Ainslie in *All, or Nothing*, and later in the
remarkable extended dream, seemingly both
telepathic and premonitory, which precipitates
three weeks of brain fever in the heroine of *A
Stern Chase* (1886), perhaps under the influence of
a temporary transmigration of her soul into her
brother's body (or of his into hers). That Mrs
Hoey believed in the possibility of such experiences
is borne out by her letters to Rosa Praed, in
connexion with Mrs Praed's 'spiritualist' novel
Nyria (1904).[24]

One of the major weaknesses of Mrs Hoey's
novels is their frequent plundering of other
people's travel-books for local colour, and often
indeed for considerable wordage. (It is obviously
no coincidence that at the time when her novels

were written she was chief reviewer of travel books for both the *Spectator* and *Chambers's Journal*.) In *Falsely True* the long and lurid episode set in Brazil relies for its evocation of that country on extensive quotations from a book by St Hilaire. Sir Charles Dilke's *Greater Britain* supplies the extensive descriptions of Ceylon in *All, or Nothing*, W.H. Russell's despatches from the Crimea and Westgarth's history of Victoria are heavily drawn on for the two exotic settings in *The Lover's Creed*, and Walter Goodman's *The Pearl of the Antilles* effectually provides the whole setting and many of the characters and incidents for the first volume of *A Stern Chase*. All of these borrowings are acknowledged in the novels, but only Goodman seems to have been applied to beforehand for permission to quote from his book. Writing to Dilke just after the publication of *All, or Nothing*, Mrs Hoey hoped that he would not be 'annoyed' with her for having borrowed 'without leave, but not without acknowledgment', from his *Greater Britain*; she conceded that perhaps she ought to have asked for his permission, but she had not liked to trouble him:[25] a surprisingly casual attitude to plagiarism in an author who showed herself, both in the Yates affair and in her dealings with publishers towards the end of her life, so anxious to receive proper credit and reward for her work.

I have already mentioned Mrs Hoey's practice of alluding to the novels of Jane Austen, Dickens, Trollope, and Thackeray for parallels to her own characters and situations. Of these novelists, only Trollope can be regarded as having significantly 'influenced' her own art. In their general shape, her plots are in the Dickensian tradition as modified by the sensation novelists of the 1860s, and her occasional use of multiple narrators, notably in *Griffith's Double*, is presumably in imitation of Wilkie Collins. The likenesses she draws attention to between her characters and those of Jane Austen or Thackeray usually appear slight and coincidental,

and there is little in common between her staple
plot materials and theirs. Trollope's novels, on
the other hand, seem to have provided specific
models or points of departure for a number of her
own plots and subplots. In the short story 'Esau's
Choice', the heroine has been reading Trollope's
Sir Harry Hotspur of Humblethwaite ('the most
melancholy of [his] fictions, with the exception of
his *Macdermots of Ballycloran*'), and throughout the
story her fate, after being jilted by her lover, is
measured against that of Trollope's heroine. In
The Question of Cain a party of ladies are robbed
of their jewels; the mastermind behind the robbery
has been a guest at the same house-party as the
ladies; and one lady in the novel refers to family
jewels as part of a wife's 'paraphernalia': all
these details closely and unmistakably recall
Trollope's *The Eustace Diamonds*. In *Out of Court*,
the villain is likened to George Vavasour, the
villain of Trollope's *Can You Forgive Her?*, but
his real prototype in that novel is Burgo
Fitzgerald, whose tactics in trying to estrange
Lady Glencora Palliser from her sobersided husband
he copies in almost every detail (and with
ultimate success): luring her into a flirtation,
persuading her to waltz outrageously with him at a
ball - to the consternation of her husband (a public
man like Palliser) who comes to take her home at the
height of her excitement - and relying on the
husband's anger and the wife's wounded pride to send
her fleeing into his more welcoming arms. It comes
as no surprise, in the light of such borrowings, to
learn that Mrs Hoey wrote one of the first major
critical articles on Trollope, 'The Novels of Mr.
Anthony Trollope', *Dublin Review*, October 1872.[26]

Although all, or nearly all,[27] of Mrs Hoey's
novels were serialized before being published in
three-volume form, and most subsequently appeared
in one-volume editions, it is clear that she
never succeeded in making a living out of them.
The publisher Tinsley stated that in 1870 his rate

of payment to Mrs Hoey for a novel was less than
£200, presumably for book rights only;[28] assuming
that serial rights brought her in no more than
another £200,[29] her total return on a novel was
probably £400 at the most. As she produced on
average one novel every two years, her annual
income from this source probably seldom exceeded
£200, unless (as seems unlikely) her popularity
increased after 1870. During the period when all
her novels appeared, 1868-90, she also contributed
stories to magazines, but not with great
frequency. Her receipts from this source probably
made only a marginal addition to her total income:
the publisher Richard Bentley's Author's Ledger
shows that she received only £13/10/- for 'The
Heiress of Moate' and £9/10/- for 'A Modern
Vendetta', both published in *Temple Bar*; for a
four-part novella and a two-part story published
in *Chambers's Journal* in 1865 she received a total
of £31/15/-, for a two-part story in 1867, £12/6/-,
for a novella in five chapters in 1868, £28/5/-,
for a novella in three chapters in 1869, £20, and
finally for a two-part story in 1874, £11/5/-.[30]

In the 1870s and 1880s, however, Mrs Hoey
probably made as much from other forms of literary
activity as the £200 or so a year from her fiction.
Bentley paid her as much as £60 for her
translations of French books, of which she
produced, on average, more than one a year
throughout the 1870s and 1880s (some of them in
collaboration with John Lillie). For her
translation of *The Correspondence of Prince
Talleyrand and King Louis XVIII* (1881), which had
to be done at breakneck speed, Bentley agreed to
pay her no less than 140 guineas (70 guineas per
volume), though in the event she was unable to
carry out the work quickly enough and received only
£40 for translating the first volume, the second
being assigned to another translator.[31] In 1892
The Author described Mrs Hoey as 'the best
translator living',[32] and her services remained in

demand in the 1890s and into the early 1900s, well after she had ceased writing novels. For Bentley, and later for Edmund Downey (Downey and Ward), Mrs Hoey also from time to time read manuscripts, though her income from this source must have been minute. And the Bentley Archives show that as well she sometimes 'revised' or 'edited' other people's novels, translations, or articles.[33] But her most regular and assured sources of income for most of her working life were almost certainly the fortnightly 'Lady's Letter' that she contributed to *The Australasian* (Melbourne) from 1874 till shortly before her death - and her reviews, subleaders, and pars in *The Spectator*, which probably began to appear in 1861 or earlier and which continued until 1895. During the years covered by the editor, Richard Hutton's 'Record of Articles' in *The Spectator* (1874-7 and 1880-97),[34] Mrs Hoey had at least one and often two contributions in most numbers, though with frequent breaks -

presumably when she was overseas or out of London; if her output during these years was typical, her income from *The Spectator* can hardly have been much less than £100 per year. As well as her 'Lady's Letter' for *The Australasian*, Mrs Hoey for many years reviewed the Royal Academy and other exhibitions of paintings for the paper: in August 1902, when she had to give the job up because she could no longer 'stand the fatigue of the Press Views', it had been contributing an extra £40 per year to her income.[35]

The Bentley Archives include a report by Geraldine Jewsbury on a novel submitted for publication by Mrs Hoey in December 1871. Entitled *Chapter and Verse*, the novel struck Jewsbury as 'clever' but 'dry', 'not entertaining'. She complained of too much 'description', and a too tangled plot with too many 'loose ends . . . from the Past'. Without having read the manuscript right through, she recommended that Bentley refuse it.[36] Except for

the tangled plot, the faults noted by Jewsbury are
hardly typical of Mrs Hoey's published novels, but
they can be found in one, *The Blossoming of an Aloe*,
which was serialized in late 1874 and published in
book form, not by Bentley, in 1875. The rejection
of the novel by Bentley, with whom she had a
connexion of several years' standing, must have been
a severe blow to Mrs Hoey, at a time when she was
beginning to establish herself as a novelist. She
must have been similarly dismayed when, a few years
later, Chambers rejected her 'French adventure',
Piccolo, for publication in *Chambers's Journal*,
accusing her of 'padding', and compounding the
insult with some rather heavy facetiousness.[37]

    With an income from her literary labours of
probably £400 or more, in addition to what her
husband earned as a barrister and journalist, and
as Secretary to the Agent-General for Victoria, it
is not immediately apparent why Mrs Hoey was always
short of money. But the remark of a writer in *The
Author* that she was 'generous to a fault' may
point to the explanation. Charity is one of the
cardinal virtues of all her more exemplary
heroines, and her own commitment to it is shown by
her writings for various charitable causes. The
dedication of her novel *All, or Nothing* also
suggests that, as well as her two daughters (until
their marriages in the 1870s), her household
included her husband's mother, who died in 1878.
She probably contributed, in addition, to the
support of her own mother, who did not die until
1890. After her husband's death, and until her
own, she continued to provide for a distant
relative of his who had no real claim on either of
them.

    Whatever its causes, her relative poverty
seems to have left her no alternative but to beg
for any scraps of work that publishers could spare
her and to continue slaving away at her desk
regardless of personal griefs (such as those

occasioned by the deaths, in 1878, of both her elder
daughter and her mother-in-law) and frequent illness
(headache, flu, eyestrain, fever, depression). At a
time when her earnings must have been near their
peak, Bentley twice had to write off money advanced
to her, under the heading of 'bad and doubtful
debts';[38] and Chambers had to threaten her with
legal action to recover £20 which she owed him when
she abruptly stopped contributing to *Chambers's
Journal*.[39] The protracted illness and expensive
surgery that preceded her husband's death at the
beginning of 1892 probably delivered the coup de
grace to their already tottering fortunes. Later
in 1892 she was voted a Civil list pension of £50
a year.

As far as I can ascertain Mrs Hoey published
no more fiction of any consequence after her
husband's death, and her output of translations,
reviews and other journalistic pieces gradually
declined during the 1890s. Her last translation,
unsigned, appeared in 1901, and apart from
occasional contributions to *The World* and her
'Lady's Letter' in *The Australasian* I have found
nothing that she published after the turn of the
century. New, revised editions of two of her
novels, *Falsely True* and *The Question of Cain*, had
been issued by Ward and Downey in 1890, after John
Cashel Hoey had bought back the copyright from
Tinsley. Subsequently however, the copyright was
sold to R.E. King Ltd when the partnership between
Ward and Downey was dissolved, and in 1900 Mrs
Hoey had the mortification of seeing King's new
editions of the two novels on sale and receiving
none of the proceeds herself - even though she
insisted that she and her husband had never
relinquished the copyright to Downey.[40] This was
only one of several fiascos arising from her
efforts to ensure that she would profit by any
revival of interest in her fiction. In a letter
to Downey on 10 February 1900, after complaining
angrily because he had sought a second opinion as

to the wisdom of publishing her proposed translation of Balzac's letters, she asserted that his firm had prevented her from 'securing [her] novels from extinction, by telling her for years that they were considering republishing them. Five days later, on her seventieth birthday, she retracted the charge to the extent of exonerating Downey from personal blame, but for the next few years her letters repeatedly take him to task for his dilatoriness: in refusing to make a firm decision to republish *The Blossoming of an Aloe* and *No Sign*, in failing to respond to Mrs Hoey's subsequent plan to offer *A House of Cards* and *No Sign* to Collins, and then in failing – and apparently being finally unable – to produce the plates and unsold copies of the two books, for which, along with the copyright, Mrs Hoey had paid £30 in 1900 and which were supposed to be in Downey's keeping. As late as August 1904, she overdrew at her bank in order to purchase the copyright, and some plates, moulds, or unsold copies, of three of her books, *A Stern Chase*, *Our of Court*, and a *Golden Sorrow*.[41] But apart from King's 'vile edition (*without a date*)' of *Falsely True* and *The Question of Cain*, none of her novels appears to have been reissued after 1890.

Consenting to read a manuscript Downey had been sent by a tyro novelist, she commented ruefully: 'The faint remembrance of the little bit of success I had in the years that are now a dream, makes me feel keenly for a woman's failure to get a hearing for what has cost the effort implied by the writing of a novel.'[42] That was in 1895, when she was 65. As she approached and passed her seventieth birthday, she became increasingly sensitive to the disrespectful neglect she felt she suffered at the hands of Downey and Co and to the slights of former friends and protegés of hers and her husband's. In the latter category, the failure of T.P. O'Connor even to reply to her request for work on his new paper *T.P.'s Weekly*, established in 1902, rankled for years.[43]

Mrs Hoey's letters to Downey, which ceased three years before her death, were written from various lodging houses in London; from various addresses in Bath, including those of friends' houses; from Boulogne or other places in France (where she spent part of the summers of 1900, 1901, 1903, and 1904); from the houses of her younger daughter or other members of her family in Ireland; and from various addresses in Malvern, which she had begun to visit with her husband some time before his death. Part of the attraction of both Bath and Malvern appears to have been their neighbouring Benedictine monasteries. Her death took place at Beccles in Suffolk on 9 July 1908, but how long she had resided there I have not been able to discover. She was buried, according to *DNB*, in the churchyard of the Benedictine church at Little Malvern. The net value of her personal estate was £19/4/-.

(Note. Since completing the above account of Mrs Hoey's life and work, I have come upon eight manuscript letters she wrote to the novelist and publisher Grant Richards during the last three years of her life. These show that despite continual bouts of illness she was still reviewing books for *The World* as late as the beginning of 1908, the year of her death. The letters, along with Richards's letters to her, are in *The Archives of Grant Richards*: see below, p.62. I have also come upon a letter to Mrs Hoey from the publishers Swan Sonnenschein and Co., dated 29 September 1899, rejecting a manuscript by Mrs Hoey entitled *Coercion*: if this was a novel, it presumably indicates that Mrs Hoey persevered with fiction for some considerable time after the publication of *His Match, and More* [1890], which appears to have been her last published novel or novella. *The Archives of Swan Sonnenschein* are also listed on p.62 below.)

[1]She recalled the event in an unpublished letter to the publisher Edmund Downey, 12 January [?1903 ?1904]. Her letters to Downey are in the National Library of Ireland. MSS 10,028,1-2.

[2]*DNB* gives 14 Feb 1830 as her date of birth, but in a letter to Downey dated 15 Feb 1900 she states that she had turned 70 that day.

[3]Before 1869 the Hoeys were not listed in the London Post Office Directory, presumably because they were not 'householders' until their move to Campden Hill Road. The Authors' Ledgers of the publishers W. and R. Chambers - among the Chambers Papers on temporary deposit in the National Library of Scotland (TD 1709) - show that Mrs Hoey lived at 18 Denbigh Street, Pimlico from Jan 1865 to July 1867, at various other lodgings from Jan 1868 to the end of May 1868, and at Campden Hill Road from some time in June 1868.

[4]Letter to Downey, undated.

[5]Her letters to Downey (1887-1905) and to the publisher Bentley (1871-[?1894]) are often dated from French addresses, as is her 'Lady's Letter' in the *Australasian* (1873-[?1908]).

[6]The fatalism of the sensation novel was denounced in a controversial lecture by the Archbishop of York. See the *Times*, 4 Nov 1864, p.6.

[7]In my bibliography of Edmund Yates, I refer to only two accounts by Escott: in his books *Masters of English Journalism* (1911) and *Anthony Trollope* (1913). I have since come across a third: in his *Great Victorians* (1916), p.347.

[8]Letters to Downey, 30 June and 7 July 1894.

[9]Letter to Downey, postmarked 13 Sep [?1900].

[10]Letters to Downey, 13 Nov [?1900] and 5 Feb [?1901].

[11]Letter to Downey, 13 Nov [?1900].

[12]Letters to Downey, 5 Feb [?1901], 4 Jan 1901, and undated [second half of 1902].

[13]*Twenty Years Ago*, p.46.

[14]Letter to Downey, undated [?Feb 1905].

[15] E.A. Baker, who wrote an introduction to the 1904 reprint, said nothing about Mrs Hoey's supposed joint-authorship of the novel.

[16] Letter to Downey, 13 Sep [?1900].

[17] Tinsley's *Recollections* were not widely noticed, and few of the notices commented on his charges against Yates and Mrs Hoey. One that did - sceptically - appeared in the *Pall Mall Gazette*, 31 Oct 1900, p.1, over the signature 'W.F.W.'. Among other embarrassing questions it asked why, if Mrs Hoey could write 'remunerative "Yates"', she could only write 'unsuccessful "Hoey"'. A more guarded reference to the matter occurs at the end of the *Spectator* review of Tinsley's book (17 Nov 1900, p.718): 'He who sells an old book as a new one; he who undertakes a collaboration, leaves the whole of the work to his partner, but lets his sole name appear on the title page; and he who takes money for work that he never performs are "rogues in grain".' It was natural that the *Spectator* should condemn Yates and side with Mrs Hoey, who until recently had been on its own staff.

[18] *Some Victorian Women*, p.9.

[19] On 8 Apr 1871 Mrs Hoey wrote to George Bentley, publisher of *Temple Bar*: '<u>Strictly private</u>./ My dear Mr. Bentley,/ I am going to Paris, on a mission for a friend of mine - to rescue papers of immense importance. <u>No one in the world knows I am going.</u> I shall [?contrive] to see a good deal. Keep a little space in *Temple Bar* for May, but do not tell any one by whom it is filled.' (Mrs Hoey's underlining) Articles on the Paris commune by Mrs Hoey did subsequently appear in the *Spectator* and *Saint Pauls*, but none in *Temple Bar*.

[20] Trollope, *The Claverings* (1867).

[21] Trollope, *An Autobiography* (1883). World's Classics paperback edition, 1980, p.156.

[22] Cf. 'A Lady's Letter from London', *The Australasian*, 5 Sep 1903, p.558.

[23] Letter from T.P. O'Connor to John Cashel Hoey, undated (National Library of Ireland, MSS 10,028). Vol 4 of *The Cabinet of Irish Literature*, comp. O'Connor and Charles A. Read, appeared in 1882. It includes an extract from Mrs Hoey's story *No Sign*.

[24] The eight letters, written July-Aug 1904, are among the Rosa Praed papers in the Oxley Memorial Library, Brisbane.

[25] Letter dated 14 Mar 1879. BM Add. ms. 43910, f.261.

[26] In the Wellesley Index to Victorian Periodicals, vol 2, the article is attributed to Mrs Hoey only conjecturally, but the case for believing it hers is greatly strengthened by the close, and broad, familiarity with Trollope's work that she shows in her novels.

[27] I have not found serializations of *Falsely True* (1870) or *Out of Court* (1874).

[28] Tinsley, *Random Recollections*, p.141.

[29] For the serialization of *A Golden Sorrow* in *Chambers's Journal* (21 instalments) she received a total of £185/15/-. For *The Blossoming of an Aloe* also in *Chambers's* (18 instalments), she received £134/17/-. *'CEJ* Authors' Ledgers', Chambers Papers.

[30] *The Archives of Richard Bentley and Son*. British Library. Microfilm, Cambridge: Chadwyck-Healey, 1976, Part 1, Reels 1-2. *'CEJ* Authors' Ledgers', Chambers Papers.

[31] Bentley Archives. British Library. Microfilm, Part 1, Reel 41.

[32] *The Author*, 2 (Jan 1892): 248.

[33] See below, V.ii, BOOKS . . . 'REVISED' BY FCH.

[34] I am grateful to the archivist of the *Spectator* for allowing me to consult the Record.

[35] Letter to Downey, 13 Aug 1902. See also below, VI, JOURNALISM, for details of Mrs Hoey's income from her contributions to *Chambers's Journal*, 1865-75.

[36] Bentley Archives. British Library. Part 1, Reel 48.

[37] 'Letter Book 1874-6', p.157. Chambers Papers.

[38] Bentley Archives. British Library, Microfilm, Part 1, Reel 2. Author's Ledger, vol 5, p.46.

[39] Mrs Hoey ceased contributing regularly to *Chambers's* in late 1874. In Dec 1874 Chambers rejected her review of *Dr. Livingstone's Last Journal* and in Mar 1875 both her novel, *Piccolo*, and her review of *On the Shores of Zuider Zee* (by Henry Havard). In his letter rejecting the latter he referred disapprovingly to her refusal to 'sanction editorial revisal', which all editors reserve 'the power of exercising'. No doubt Mrs Hoey began to feel discouraged. At any rate, requests from Chambers for further contributions in July and Oct 1875 elicited only one 'digest' of a travel-book (published in the journal on 23 Oct 1875). On 17 Nov 1876 Chambers wrote to Mrs Hoey demanding either repayment of £20 he had advanced Mrs Hoey or further contributions in lieu. He acknowledged receipt of the £20 on 28 March 1877. (Chambers Papers, Letter Books, 1874-6 and 1877-91.)

[40] Letters to Downey (2), undated [?early 1900].

[41] Letter to Downey, 8 Aug 1904.

[42] Letter to Downey, 11 May 1895.

[43] Letters to Downey, 1902-5, passim.

I NOVELS

A House of Cards

1   Serialized: *Tinsley's Magazine*, 2(Mar 1868)-
    4(Feb 1869).

2   First ed. *A House of Cards/ A Novel./ By/
    Mrs. Cashel Hoey.//* London: Tinsley
    Brothers, 1868. [Dedicated to 'My dear
    father, by whom it was suggested'.]

3   New ed. 1 vol. 'Select Library of Fiction'.
    Chapman and Hall, [1871]. [In a letter
    Mrs Hoey states that she 'had to compress
    the story' for this edition.]

Falsely True

4   First ed. *Falsely True./ A Novel./ By/ Mrs.
    Cashel Hoey,/ Author of 'A House of Cards,'
    etc. etc./'His honour, rooted in dishonour
    stood;/ And faith, unfaithful, kept him
    falsely true.'//* 3 vols. London: Tinsley
    Brothers, 1870. [Dedicated to James Payn.]

5   New and revised ed. 1 vol. Ward and Downey,
    1890. ['This story (first published in
    1870) is dedicated to James Payn.' The
    revisions consist chiefly of excisions of
    passages of description and authorial
    moralizing, but the ending is changed -
    decidedly for the better - by the omission
    of a final four-page section sketching the
    state of affairs six years after the
    conclusion of the main action. A number
    of minor corrections are also made.]

6   New ed. 1 vol. 'The Imperial Library',
    'The Sun Dial Library'. R.E. King Ltd,
    [?1901]. [Not sighted. Referred to in an
    undated letter from Mrs Hoey to Edmund

Downey. Listed in English Catalogue of
Books, 1901-5.]

A Golden Sorrow

7 Serialized: *Chambers's Journal*, 6 Jan 1872-
   25 May 1872. ['By the author of *A House
   of Cards*'.]

8 First ed. *A Golden Sorrow./ By/ Mrs. Cashel
   Hoey,/ Author of/ 'A House of Cards,'
   'Falsely True,'/ etc. etc./ 'I swear, 'tis
   better to be lowly born,/ And range with
   humble livers in content,/ Than to be
   perked up in a glistering grief,/ And
   wear a golden sorrow.'/ King Henry the
   Eighth.//* 3 vols. London: Hurst and
   Blackett, 1872. [Dedicated,
   'affectionately', to Jean Ingelow.]

9 2 vols. Leipzig, 1872.

10 New ed. 1 vol. Sampson, Low, 1880.

The Blossoming of an Aloe and *The Queen's Token*

11 Serialized: *The Blossoming of an Aloe,
    Chambers's Journal*, 29 Aug 1874-26 Dec
    1874.

            *The Queen's Token, London
    Society*, 25(May 1874)-26 (Sep 1874).

12 First ed. *The Blossoming of an Aloe/ And/
    The Queen's Token./ By/ Mrs. Cashel Hoey,/
    Author of/ 'Out of Court,' 'A Golden
    Sorrow,'/ etc. etc.//* 3 vols. London:
    Hurst and Blackett, 1875. [On verso of
    title page: '"She was of those who are
    content to wait for the blossoming of an
    aloe; and who do not weary of the
    hundred years." - *From Birth to Bridal*.'
    Dedication: 'These stories are dedicated
    to my Mother.']

13   New ed. *The Blossoming of an Aloe.* 1 vol.
      'The Country House Library. No. 3.'
      'Select Library of Fiction.' Ward, Lock,
      and Tyler, [1876].

14   New ed. *The Queen's Token.* 1 vol. Spencer
      Blackett, 1889. [Not sighted.]

Out of Court

15   First ed. *Out of Court./ By/ Mrs. Cashel
      Hoey,/ Author of/ 'A Golden Sorrow,' 'A
      House of Cards,'/ 'Buried in the Deep,'
      etc. etc./ 'The Gospel checks the law
      which throws the stone.'//* 3 vols.
      London: Hurst and Blackett, 1874.
      [Dedicated to the Hon. Sir Charles Gavan
      Duffy.]

16   New ed. 1 vol. 'Low's Standard Novels'.
      Sampson Low, n.d. [Not sighted. Listed
      in English Catalogue of Books, 1881-9.]

Griffith's Double

17   Serialized: *All the Year Round,* 4 Dec 1875-
      5 Aug 1876.

18   Serialized: *The Australasian* (Melbourne),
      8 Jan 1876-20 Jan 1877.

19   First ed. *Griffith's Double./ By/ Mrs.
      Cashel Hoey,/ Author of/ "A Golden Sorrow,"
      "Out of Court,"/ "The Blossoming of an
      Aloe,"/ etc. etc.//* 3 vols. London: Hurst
      and Blackett, 1876. [Dedicated to 'My
      Daughter and Her Husband'.]

All, or Nothing

20   Serialized: *All the Year Round,* 13 July
      1878-8 Mar 1879.

21   First ed. *All, or Nothing./ By/ Mrs. Cashel
      Hoey/ Author of/ 'Griffith's Double,' 'A
      Golden Sorrow,'/ 'The Blossoming of an*

*Aloe,'/ etc., etc./ 'Thou shalt have no
other gods but Me.'// 3 vols. London:
Hurst and Blackett, 1879. [Dedication:
'This story is dedicated to the beloved
and honoured memory of My Husband's Mother,
who, for twenty years, was my most constant
reader and most gentle critic; and who, to
the end, found some slight solace for pain
in its pages. May she rest in peace.']

22   New ed. 1 vol. Spencer Blackett, 1888.
      [Not sighted.]

23   New ed. 1 vol. 'Sun Dial Library'. R.E.
      King Ltd, [?————]. [Not sighted. Listed
      in English Catalogue of Books, 1901-5.]

The Question of Cain

24   Serialized: *All the Year Round*, 26 Mar 1881-
      10 Dec 1882.

25   First ed. *The Question of Cain/ By/ Mrs.
      Cashel Hoey/ Author of/ 'A Golden Sorrow,'
      'All or Nothing,'/ 'The Blossoming of an
      Aloe,'/ etc., etc./ 'Am I my Brother's
      Keeper?'//* 3 vols. London: Hurst and
      Blackett, 1882. [Dedicated to Sir John
      Pope Hennessy, Governor of Hong Kong.]

26   New and revised ed. 1 vol. Ward and Downey,
      1890. [The revision includes a number of
      corrections, stylistic improvements,
      compressions, and deletions. The title of
      the last chapter is changed from 'The Next
      of Kin' to 'Helen's Inheritance', and the
      chapter itself is substantially rewritten,
      chiefly with the object of removing some
      of the more absurd romantic improbabilities
      that mark the denouement.]

27   New ed. 1 vol. 'The Imperial Library'.
      R.E. King Ltd, [?1900]. [Not sighted.
      Referred to in letters from Mrs Hoey to
      Edmund Downey.]

The Lover's Creed

28   Serialized: *Belgravia*, 52(Jan 1884)-55 (Dec 1884)

29   First ed. *The Lover's Creed/ A Novel/ By/ Mrs. Cashel Hoey/ Author of/ 'The Question of Cain' 'The Blossoming of an Aloe' 'No Sign' etc./ 'One, and One Only, Is the Lover's Creed'/ Oliver Wendell Holmes//* 3 vols. London: Chatto and Windus, 1884. [Dedicated to the Right Hon Hugh Culling Eardley Childers, Chancellor of the Exchequer. 12 illustrations, by P. Macnab.]

30   U.S. ed. N.Y.: Harper, 1884.

31   U.S. ed. N.Y.: G. Munro, 1884.

A Stern Chase

32   Serialized: *All the Year Round*, 29 Aug 1885-1 May 1886.

33   First ed. *A Stern Chase./ A Novel./ By/ Mrs. Cashel Hoey,/ Author of 'The Lover's Creed,'/ 'The Question of Cain,' 'A Golden Sorrow,' etc./ 'A stern chase is a long chase.'//* 3 vols. London: Sampson Low, Marston, etc., 1886. [Dedicated to Robert Murray Smith, Agent General for Victoria.]

34   New ed. 1 vol. Sampson Low, 1888. [This edition is 'revised' to the extent of some minor corrections, stylistic changes - chiefly compressions - and a few brief deletions.]

His Match, and More

35   *His Match, and More*. Published as Summer Number of *Household Words*, 26 June 1890. [Not sighted.]

36 First ed. *Nazareth./ By/ Mrs. Cashel Hoey./
    With a Preface/ By the Rev. W. Humphrey,/
    Of the Congregation of the Oblates of St.
    Charles.//* 1 vol. London: Burns and
    Oates, 1873. [On verso of title page, a
    'Nihil obstat' granted by Francis Wyndham,
    censor deputatus of the Congregation of the
    Oblates of St Charles, and the 'Imprimatur' of
    Henry Edward [Manning], Archbishop of
    Westminster. The book is an account, 79pp.
    long, of the 'charitable labours of the
    religious ladies of Nazareth [i.e. the
    Congregation of Nazareth, a French order] for
    the spiritual and moral welfare of the women
    of Galilee'. It consists of translations,
    from the French, of letters addressed by one
    of the ladies to her pupils in France.]

III SHORTER FICTION

37 'Buried in the Deep', *Chambers's Journal*, 4
    Feb-25 Feb 1865. [Unsigned. Probably Mrs
    Hoey's first published work of fiction. A
    sensational novella in four chapters.]

38 '57 Chandos Street, S.W.', *Chambers's
    Journal*, 16-23 Sep 1865. [Unsigned. A
    half-hearted sensation story, in two parts.]

39 'A Shot in the Scrub', *Chambers's Journal*, 19-
    26 Jan 1867. [Unsigned. A rather
    unconvincing tale of bushrangers in Tasmania;
    in two parts.]

40 ''The Heiress of Moate', *Temple Bar*, 19(Mar
    1867):493-519. ['By the Author of the "Iron
    Casket".' Signed at end: 'Frances Cashel

Hoey.' Presumably 'The Iron Casket' was a
short story or novella: I have not found
it.]

41   'The Mystery of Pegwell Place', *Chambers's
      Journal*, 4-25 Apr 1868. [Unsigned.
      Another mildly sensational novella; in four
      parts (but five chapters).]

42   'The Brown Lady', *Belgravia*, 8(Mar-Apr 1869):
      53-69, 197-219. ['By Mrs. Cashel Hoey,
      Author of "A House of Cards," "The Iron
      Casket," etc.']

43   'Roberts's Capital Hit', *Chambers's Journal*,
      3-17 July 1869. [Unsigned. In three parts.]

44   'A Modern Vendetta', *Temple Bar*, 30(Nov 1870):
      471-489). [Unsigned.]

45   *Buried in the Deep, and Other Tales* [?   ]:
      [?Smith and Son], [?1871]. [Not sighted.
      Not in BM Cat. A Letter from W. & R.
      Chambers to FCH, dated 8 June 1871, gave
      Smith and Son permission to republish stories
      which had previously appeared in *Chambers's
      Journal* (W. & R. Chambers papers, 'Letter
      Book 1868-83', p.153). Smith may have been
      a Dublin or provincial publisher.]

46   New ed. London: Chapman and Hall, 1873. [Not
      sighted. Not in BM Cat. The book is listed
      in ECB and was reviewed in the *Spectator*, 8
      Feb 1873, p.184. The new ed., but not any
      first ed., is mentioned among FCH's books in
      her entry in *Who Was Who*. The title story
      was reprinted from *Chambers's Journal* (see
      item 37, above). Two other stories named in
      the *Spectator* review are 'A Shot in the
      Scrub' (also rpt. from *Chambers's Journal*)
      and 'Dulcie's Delusion'.]

47   'The Story of Burton's Loan', *Chambers's
      Journal*, 14-21 Feb 1874. [Unsigned. In two
      parts.]

48   *No Sign,/ and Other Tales./ By/ Mrs. Cashel
      Hoey,/ Author of/ 'The Blossoming of an
      Aloe,' 'A Golden Sorrow,' etc.//* 'The
      Country House Library. No. 5.' 1 vol.
      London: Ward, Lock, and Tyler, [1876].
      [Dedicated to Mrs John Aloysius Blake.
      Contents: 'Only an Episode' (rpt. from
      New Quarterly Magazine, 4, Apr 1875);
      'Dark Cybel' (rpt. from *ibid*, 4, July
      1875); 'No Sign' (rpt. from *ibid*, 5,Oct
      1875).]

49   'Kate Cronin's Dowry', *New Quarterly
      Magazine*, 7(Jan 1877):472-501. [Signed.]

50   ――――――. N.Y.: Harper & Bros., 1877.
      [Not sighted. Listed in *L of C Cat*.]

51   'From the Cliff's Edge', *All the Year Round*,
      Extra Summer Number, 2 July 1877, pp.36-45.
      [Signed.]

52   'Ralph Craven's Silver Whistle', in *Wit and
      Pleasure: Seven Tales by Seven Authors*.
      1 vol. Seven illustrations. London:
      Virtue, 1877, pp.79-112. [Signed. This
      story, a semi-historical romance, is set
      in Ireland.]

53   'Esau's Choice', *New Quarterly Magazine*, 9
      (Jan 1878):299-323. [Signed.]

54   'Proctor's Case', *All the Year Round*, Extra
      Summer Number, 1 July 1878, pp.52-64.
      [Signed.]

55   'Pompey's Peril'. London: Society for the
      Protection of Animals from Vivisection,
      [?1883]. [Not sighted. Reviewed in the
      Spectator, 56 (3 Feb 1883):158-9, where it
      is described as having been 'written for
      the *Zoophilist*'.]

56   'A Case of Delusion', *All the Year Round*,
      Extra Summer Number, 17 June 1889, pp.1-12.
      [Signed.]

57   'The Damaris Cot', in *In a Good Cause; a Collection of Stories*. [Souvenir of a performance given on Thurs, 3 May 1900, in aid of Mr Punch's fund for the Hospital for Sick Children, Great Ormond Street. Not sighted.]

IV CONTRIBUTIONS TO BOOKS

58   'Philanthropic Work of Women in British Colonies and the East', in *Woman's Mission; a Series of Congress Papers on the Philanthropic Work of Women, by Eminent Writers*, ed. the Baroness Burdett-Coutts. London: Sampson Low, 1893, pp.334-360. [A factual account, based mainly on reports by government departments and religious bodies – Anglican and Roman Catholic – and dealing chiefly with the Australian colonies, especially Victoria.]

59   Carleton, William. *The Life of William Carleton: Being His Autobiography and Letters; and an Account of His Life and Writings, from the Point at Which the Autobiography Breaks Off, by David J. O'Donoghue*. 'With an Introduction by Mrs Cashel Hoey.' 2 vols. London: Downey & Co., 1896. [Mrs Hoey's Introduction occupies nearly 50pp.]

i Translations

60   [Anon.] *The Life of Madame de la Rochefoucauld, Duchesse de Doudeauville, Foundress of the Society of Nazareth.* 'Translated from French by Mrs. Cashel Hoey, Author of "Nazareth," etc. etc.' 1 vol. London: Burns and Oates, 1878. ['The English Version of this Book Is Inscribed to The beloved Memory of Charlotte Murray Stewart, Child of Mary of Nazareth.' Charlotte Stewart was presumably one of Mrs Hoey's two daughters by her first marriage.]

61   [Anon.] *What Might Have Been.* 'From the French by Mrs. Cashel Hoey.' 1 vol. London: Burns and Oates, 1881. [It is just conceivable that this novel, a heavily pious tale set mainly in the period between the Franco-Prussian war and the Paris commune, is not really a translation but an original work by Mrs Hoey herself.]

62   Biart, Lucien. *An Involuntary Voyage.* 'Translated by Mrs. Cashel Hoey and Mr. John Lillie.' 1 vol. London: Sampson Low, Marston, etc., 1880.

63   ——————. *The Clients of Doctor Bernagius.* 'From the French of M. Lucien Biart by Mrs. Cashel Hoey.' 1 vol. London: Sampson Low, Marston, etc., 1881. [With a preface by 'The Translator', pp. iii-vi.]

64   Bourgeois, Emile. *The Century of Louis XIV; Its Arts - Its Ideas.* 'From the French of Émile Bourgeois, Lecturer at the École Normale Supérieure, of Paris,

by Mrs. Cashel Hoey.' 1 vol. London:
Sampson Low, Marston, n.d. [?1896].

65   Bourget, Paul. *André Cornelis*. 'Translated
       from the French of Paul Bourget by Mrs.
       Cashel Hoey . . . .' 1 vol. London:
       Spencer Blackett, n.d. [?1888].

66   Broglie, Duc de. *Frederick the Great and
       Maria Theresa. From Hitherto Unpublished
       Documents. 1740-1742.* 'From the French
       by Mrs. Cashel Hoey and Mr. John Lillie.'
       2 vols. London: Sampson Low, Marston, etc.,
       1883.

66   Célières, Paul. *The Startling Exploits of
       Dr. J.B. Quies.* 'From the French of Paul
       Célières by Mrs. Cashel Hoey and Mr. John
       Lillie.' 1 vol. London: Sampson Low, 1886.

67   Challamel, Augustin. *The History of Fashion
       in France; or, The Dress of Women from the
       Gallo-Roman Period to the Present Time.*
       'From the French of M. Augustin Challamel
       by Mrs. Cashel Hoey and Mr. John Lillie.'
       1 vol. London: Sampson Low, Marston, etc.,
       1882.

68   Champfleury, M. (pseud. of Jules François
       Fleury-Husson). *The Cat Past and Present.*
       'From the French of M. Champfleury with
       Supplementary Notes by Mrs. Cashel Hoey.'
       1 vol. London: George Bell, 1885. [Opens
       with 'A Few Words to the Reader', signed
       'Frances Cashel Hoey. September 1884', in
       which Mrs Hoey mentions her own 'home
       circle' of cats - 'the cats, in fact, to
       whom we belong'.]

69   Claretie, Jules. *Camille Desmoulins and
       His Wife; Passages from the History of
       the Dantonists, Founded upon New and
       Hitherto Unpublished Documents.*
       'Translated from the French of Jules
       Claretie by Mrs. Cashel Hoey'. 1 vol.

London: Smith, Elder, 1876.

70   Daudet, Ernest. *Rafael, a Romance of the
      History of Spain*. 'From the French of M.
      Ernest Daudet by Mrs. Cashel Hoey.' 1 vol.
      London: Sampson Low, Marston, etc., 1896.

71   Erckmann[Emile]-Chatrian[Pierre Alexandre],
      MM. *The Outbreak of the Great French
      Revolution, Related by a Peasant of
      Lorraine*. 'Translated by Mrs. Cashel Hoey.'
      3 vols. London: Bentley, 1871.

72   Figuier, L. *The Day after Death, or, Our
      Future Life according to Science*.
      Translated from the French of Louis Figuier.
      1 vol. London: Bentley, 1872. [No
      translator's name appears on the title page,
      but FCH is identified as the translator in
      the Bentley Archives and Publications Lists.
      The original title was *Le Lendemain de la
      Mort*. The work was slightly abridged in
      translation.]

73   Fleury, Maurice de. *Medicine and the Mind*.
      (*La Médecine de l'esprit.*). 'Translated
      . . . by S.B. Collins, M.D.' London: Downey
      and Co., 1900. [Mrs Hoey's name was
      omitted from the title page at her own
      request, but her correspondence with Downey
      reveals that she was joint-translator; her
      colleague (Dr Stacy Collins) was apparently
      less proficient in French than in medicine.]

74   Fleury, Maurice de. *The Criminal Mind. From
      the French*. London: Downey and Co., 1901.
      [Mrs Hoey's name does not appear as
      translator, but her correspondence with
      Downey reveals that she did translate the
      work - first published in French in 1898.]

75   Gaulot, Paul. *A Friend of the Queen (Marie
      Antoinette - Count de Fersen)*. 'From the
      French of Paul Gaulot by Mrs. Cashel Hoey.'
      2 vols. London: Heinemann, 1894.

76   Goblet, Eugène (Comte d'Alviella). *Sahara and Lapland. Travels in the African Desert and the Polar World.* 'Translated from the French by Mrs. Cashel Hoey.' 1 vol. London: Asher & Co., 1874.

77   Havard, Henry. *The Heart of Holland.* 'Translated by Mrs. Cashel Hoey.' 1 vol. London: Bentley, 1880.

78   D'Héricault, Charles. *1794. A Tale of the Terror.* 'From the French of M. Charles D'Héricault by Mrs. Cashel Hoey.' 1 vol. Dublin: M.H. Gill, 1884. [A preface by Mrs Hoey, pp.v-ix, indicates that the French title of the book was *Les Aventures de deux Parisiennes pendant la Terreur.* Its author, Mrs Hoey says, 'holds a high rank among contemporary French writers'.]

79   Humbert, Aimé. *Japan and the Japanese.* 'Translated by Mrs. Cashel Hoey and Edited by H.W. Bates.' 1 vol. London: Bentley, 1874.

80   Lenoir, Paul. *The Fayoun, or Artists in Egypt.* 1 vol. London: Henry S. King, 1873. [Mrs Hoey is identified as the translator in the publisher's list at the end of the volume (p.3), but her name does not appear on the title page.]

81   de Melito, Count Miot. *Memoirs of Count Miot de Melito, Councillor of State, and Member of the Institute of France, between the Years 1788 and 1815,* edited by General Fleischmann. 'From the French by Mrs. Cashel Hoey and Mr. John Lillie.' 2 vols. London: Sampson Low, Marston, etc., 1881.

82   Neukomm, Edmond. *Tamers of the Sea; the Northmen in America from the Tenth to the Fifteenth Century.* 'From the French of M. Edmond Neukomm by Mrs. Cashel Hoey.' 1 vol. London: Sampson Low, 1897.

83   Ohnet, Georges. *Dr. Rameau*. 'Translated by
      Mrs. Cashel Hoey.' 1 vol. London: Chatto
      and Windus, 1889.

84   Plon, Eugène. *Thorvaldsen; His Life and Works*.
      'Translated by Mrs. Cashel Hoey.' 1 vol.
      London: Bentley, 1874.

85   Rabbe, Félix. *Shelley, the Man and the Poet*.
      From the French. 2 vols. London: Ward and
      Downey, 1888. [FCH's name does not appear
      on the title-page. The translation is
      attributed to her by J.F. Kirk (Supplement
      to *Allibone's Critical Dictionary* . . .).]

86   de Rémusat, Mme. *Memoirs of Madame de
      Rémusat. 1802-1808. Published by Her
      Grandson, M. Paul de Rémusat*. 'Translated
      from the French by Mrs. Cashel Hoey and Mr.
      John Lillie.' 2 vols. London: Sampson Low,
      1880.

87   ──────────. New ed. 1 vol. Sampson Low,
      [?1895]. [The British Library copy is
      stamped 1895, but the book was printed in
      America, 'Copyright 1879, by D. Appleton &
      Co.'.]

88   ──────────. *A Selection from the Letters of
      Mme. de Rémusat to Her Husband and Son,
      from 1804 to 1813*. 'From the French by
      Mrs. Cashel Hoey and Mr. John Lillie.'
      London: Sampson Low, 1881.

89   Robida, A. *Yester-year; Ten Centuries of
      Toilette*. 'From the French of A. Robida
      by Mrs. Cashel Hoey.' 1 vol. London:
      Sampson Low, 1892.

90   Simon, Jules. *The Government of M. Thiers
      from 8th February 1871 to 24th May 1873*.
      From the French. 2 vols. London: Sampson
      Low, 1879. [FCH's name does not appear on
      the title-page. The translation is
      attributed to her in Mary Furlong and
      Douglas Hyde, eds., *Irish Literature*, 4:1578.]

91   [Talleyrand.] *The Correspondence of Prince
      Talleyrand and King Louis XVIII during the
      Congress of Vienna.* . . . 'With a Preface,
      Observations, and Notes by M.G. Pallain.'
      2 vols. London: Bentley, 1881. [No
      translator's name appears on the title-page,
      but the Bentley Archives and Publications
      List indicates that FCH translated the first
      volume and Mrs M.C.M. Simpson (née Senior)
      the second. See INTRODUCTION, above.]

92   Verne, Jules. *For the Flag.* 'From the French
      of Jules Verne by Mrs. Cashel Hoey.' 1 vol.
      London: Sampson Low, 1897.

93   ——————. *An Antarctic Mystery.* 'Translated
      by Mrs Cashel Hoey.' 1 vol. London: Sampson
      Low, 1898.

                   ii 'Revisions'

94   Corvin[-Wiersbitzki], Colonel Otto. *In France
      with the Germans.* 2 vols. London: Bentley,
      1872.   FCH's name does not appear on the
      title-page, but the Author's Ledgers among
      the Bentley Archives record that she was
      paid £25 for 'revising' the work. At this
      price, the revision would have been very
      extensive.]

95   [?] Clarke, Marcus. *His Natural Life.* 3 vols.
      London: Bentley, 1875. [FCH corrected the
      proofs of the novel on Clarke's behalf and *may*
      have been responsible for the extensive, mainly
      minor revisions that were made for the first
      English edition. See my note, 'The English
      Publication of *His Natural Life*', *Australian
      Literary Studies*, 10 (Oct 1982):520-6.]

96   Mathers, Helen (Mrs Reeves). *Cherry Ripe.* 3 vols.
      London: Bentley, 1878. [Three letters from FCH

                          50

to George Bentley in the Bentley Archives
indicate that she extensively revised the
novel for its publication in book-form.
It had previously been serialized in *Temple
Bar*, published by Bentley, 49(Jan 1877)-52
(Jan 1878).]

97   [Willard, Mrs F.J.]   *Pictures from Paris
      in War and in Siege*. By an American Lady.
      1 vol. London: Bentley, 1871. [FCH's name
      does not appear on the title-page, but the
      Author's Ledgers among the Bently Archives
      record that she was paid £10 for 'revising'
      the work. At this price it must have
      required fairly extensive revision.]

                    VI JOURNALISM

              i Journals to which FCH
                contributed regularly
                [In alphabetical order]

98   *The Australasian* (Melbourne). [Mrs Hoey began
      contributing 'A Lady's Letter from London'
      (unsigned) to the paper's 'Society and
      Fashion' column on 31 May 1873 and continued
      to do so, at intervals varying from weekly
      to four-weekly, until at least August 1904
      and possibly until her death in July 1908.
      (The column continued, in the same style,
      after her death.) Occasionally her column
      was titled 'A Lady's Letter from Home' or,
      as appropriate, 'A Lady's Letter from Paris',
      'Dublin', 'Boulogne', 'Oberammagau', etc.
      See INTRODUCTION.]

99   *Chambers's Journal*. [See also INTRODUCTION
      and III SHORTER FICTION. *DNB* states that
      Mrs Hoey wrote constantly for *Chambers's*
      between 1865 and 1894. In fact her first
      contribution appeared on 28 Jan 1865 and her

last on 23 Oct 1875. During this period
she contributed a total of 78 articles, 6
novellas, and 2 novels. Most of her articles
were reviews - or, as Chambers more
accurately called them, 'digests' - of travel
books. In the period 1865-9 her
contributions averaged between 12 and 13 a
year, for which she received an average of
about £55 a year. In the period 1870-5 her
contributions were much less numerous but
included the two novels *A Golden Sorrow* and
The Blossoming of an Aloe. For her shorter
contributions (averaging 6 a year), she
received an average of about £22 a year.
Information from the *Chambers's Edinburgh
Journal* 'Author's Ledgers', on temporary
deposit in the National Library of Scotland.]

100   *The Dublin Review* [See also INTRODUCTION. *The
Wellesley Index to Victorian Periodicals*
lists 11 contributions by FCH, some of them
conjectural and some probably or certainly
written in collaboration with her husband,
who was subeditor of the magazine from 1865
to 1879. An article, 'Additions and
Corrections to the *Wellesley Index* for *The
Dublin Review*, Jan 1864-July 1900', by Ann
Palmer (*Victorian Periodicals Review*, 15,
Spring 1982:30-37), conjecturally adds two
more articles probably written by FCH in
collaboration with her husband.]

101   *The Freeman's Journal* (Dublin). [Not sighted.
According to *DNB*, FCH began contributing
'reviews and articles on art' in 1853. Her
contributions probably ceased when she left
Dublin in late 1855 or early 1856.]

102   *The Morning Post* (London). [Not sighted.
According to *DNB*, FCH began contributing
reviews to the paper when she first went to
London in late 1855 or early 1856.]

103   *The Nation* (Dublin). [See INTRODUCTION. Not
sighted.]

104   *The Spectator.* [See also INTRODUCTION. Mrs
       Hoey contributed one signed article, 'A
       Catholic Lady in "Red" Paris', 15 April 1871,
       pp. 444-6 (reprinted, unsigned, in *Littell's
       Living Age*, 109[13 May 1871]:431-6), and an
       enormous number of unsigned reviews. The
       'Record of Articles' kept by R.H. Hutton (co-
       editor of the *Spectator*) from 14 Nov 1874 to
       10 Nov 1877 and from 20 Nov 1880 till
       Hutton's death on 9 Sep 1897 shows that FCH
       was the magazine's most prolific reviewer of
       travel books in the 1870s and 1880s. She
       also contributed subleaders on a wide variety
       of topics, reviews of the 'lighter'
       magazines, and pars for the 'Current
       Literature' page. In the 1870s she seldom
       reviewed new novels (though the review of
       Rhoda Broughton's *Joan*, 30 Dec 1876, was by
       her); but in the 1880s she was frequently
       entrusted with the latest works of Payn,
       Besant, Justin McCarthy, M.E. Braddon, and
       George Moore. She also, on occasions,
       reviewed plays and exhibitions. Her last
       contribution appeared on 18 May 1895.]

105   *Temple Bar.* [See also SHORTER FICTION. In
       addition to short stories, FCH contributed
       4 reviews during the period 1873-8. She also
       'edited' two short stories published in the
       journal. Her contributions are listed in
       the *Wellesley Index to Victorian Periodicals*.]

106   *The World.* [See also INTRODUCTION. According
       to *DNB*, FCH helped Edmund Yates to 'plan'
       The World and was one of its original
       contributors in 1874. Most of her
       contributions appear to have been short,
       unsigned notices of new books for the paper's
       'Pages in Waiting' section. Many of them are
       referred to in her unpublished correspondence
       with Edmund Downey (see below, VII
       MANUSCRIPTS). She also contributed
       occasional signed articles, including one for

the 'Pages in Waiting' section, on Henry
Seton Merriman, 30 Aug 1904, p.351, which is
the latest of her literary efforts that I
have been able to trace.]

ii Other contributions
to journals
[In chronological order]

107   '"Red" Paris on Easter Sunday', *Saint Pauls*,
      8(May 1871):163-76. [Signed.]

108   'Thérèse Tietjens', *Belgravia*, 34(Nov 1877):
      70-82. [Signed.]

VII MANUSCRIPTS
[Listed alphabetically by location.]

British Library

109   ALS to Sir Charles Dilke, 14 Mar 1879. Add.
      MS 43910, f.261. [See INTRODUCTION.]

110   ALS to T.H.S. Escott, 26 Nov 1884. Escott
      papers, Add. MS 58781, ff.126-7.

National Library of Ireland

111   114 ALS, postcards, memos, reader's
      reports, and other items from Mrs Hoey to
      Edmund Downey, 1887-1905. MSS 10028, 1-2.
      [See INTRODUCTION. Enclosed with Mrs Hoey's
      letters are a letter from T.P. O'Connor to
      her husband John Cashel Hoey, n.d. (?1881);
      a letter to Mrs Hoey from the publisher
      R.B. Marston, 22 Feb 1896; and 2 typed
      letters to Mrs Hoey from the publishers
      R.E. King Ltd, 12 Sep and 15 Oct 1900.
      Attached to one of Mrs Hoey's letters is a

satirical poem, 'Mr. Rhodes to Mr. Chamberlain', n.d. (?early 1900).]

112   4 ALS. To 'Sir', 'Mr. Hall', 'Miss Penny', and 'Miss Crommelin'. MSS 13830. [None of the letters is fully dated, but three were written from 17 Campden Hill Road, Kensington, where FCH lived from early 1868 to about 1892; the fourth letter certainly belongs to the same period. A note (not in FCH's hand) attached to the letter to Miss Crommelin, dates it [?1860], but it contains what appears to be a reference to the recent death of FCH's daughter Charlotte, which occurred in 1878.

National Library of Scotland

113   2 ALS to the publisher Blackwood, 17 Aug [1866] and 3 Apr 1872. Blackwood Papers, MSS 4209, 4291. [With the second of these, FCH sent Blackwood the ms of her novel *The Queen's Token*, about which R.H. Hutton, editor of the *Spectator*, had spoken to Blackwood on her behalf. Blackwoods did not publish the novel, nor any of her others.]

Oxley Memorial Library (Brisbane)

114   8 ALS to the novelist Rosa Praed (Mrs Campbell Praed); most, if not all, written in 1904. Rosa Praed Papers. [See INTRODUCTION.]

University of Illinois Library

115   43 ALS, one telegram, one reader's report, and one memo, to the publisher Bentley, 1871- [?1894]. *The Archives of Richard Bentley and Son 1829-1898*. Microfilm, Cambridge: Chadwyck-Healey, 1976, Part II, Reel 35. [Many of the letters are undated or imperfectly dated, but a more or less precise date can be assigned to most of them on the basis of internal evidence.

Two of the letters are addressed to Richard
Bentley, the rest to his father, George
Bentley. 3 ALS from George Bentley to FCH,
relating to her translation of *The
Correspondence of Prince Talleyrand and
King Louis XVIII* (early 1881), are in the
British Library (*The Archives of Richard
Bentley*, Part I, Reel 41).]

VIII REVIEWS OF FCH'S FICTION

A House of Cards

116   *Athenaeum*, 2143(21 Nov 1868):676.   [By
       (?Romer). Unsigned.]

117   *Spectator*, 46(8 Feb 1873):184.

Falsely True

118   *Athenaeum*, 2236(3 Sep 1870):304-5. [By
       (?Romer). Unsigned.]

119   *Spectator*, 24 Sep 1870, pp.1147-9.
       [Conjecturally attributed to R.H. Hutton
       by Professor R.H. Tener: cf. *Spectator*
       reviews of *A Golden Sorrow*, *Out of Court*
       and *All, or Nothing*, below.]

A Golden Sorrow

120   *Athenaeum*, 2327(1 June 1872):685-6. [By
       (?Romer). Unsigned.]

121   *Saturday Review*, 49(22 May 1880):669-70.

122   *Spectator*, 8 June 1872, pp.725-6. [By
       R.H. Hutton?]

Buried in the Deep, and Other Tales

123   *Spectator*, 46(8 Feb 1873):184.

Out of Court

124   *Academy*, 5 (Apr 1874):424-5. [Signed A.
       Lang.]

125   *Athenaeum*, 2421 (21 Mar 1874):388. [By
       Hepworth Dixon. Unsigned.]

126   *Spectator*, 14 Mar 1874, pp.335-6. [By R.H.
       Hutton?]

127   *Times*, 21 Aug 1874, p.12.

The Blossoming of an Aloe and *The Queen's Token*

128   *Academy*, 7(13 Feb 1875):163. [Signed George
       Saintsbury.]

129   *London Society*, 27(Feb 1875):190.

130   *Spectator*, 48(2 Jan 1875):17-19. [By R.H.
       Hutton. Unsigned.]

131   —————, 63(12 Oct 1889):502.

132   *Times*, 25 Jan 1875, p. 4.

Griffith's Double

133   *Academy* (George Saintsbury), 10(16 Sep 1876):
       286.

134   *Athenaeum*, 2545(5 Aug 1876):174. [By (?-)
       Collyer. Unsigned.]

135   *New Quarterly Magazine*, 7(Oct 1876):265-6.
       [By O.J.F. Crawfurd.]

136   *Spectator*, 49(7 Oct 1876):1250-1. [By R.H.
       Hutton. Unsigned.]

All, or Nothing

137   *Academy*, 15(17 May 1879):431. [Signed
       Richard F. Littledale.]

138   *Athenaeum*, 2684(5 Apr 1879):436. [By (?-)
       Cook. Unsigned.]

139   *Spectator*, 29 Mar 1879, pp.408-9. [By R.H.
       Hutton?]

The Question of Cain

140   *Academy*, 21(28 Jan 1882):59. [Signed Leonora
       B. Lang.]

141   *Athenaeum*, 2833(11 Feb 1882):186. [By (?-)
       Collyer. Unsigned.]

142   *Graphic*, 25(18 Feb 1882):166.

143   *Spectator*, 55(18 Feb 1882):236. [By R.H.
       Hutton. Unsigned.]

The Lover's Creed

144   *Academy*, 26(13 Dec 1884):389. [Signed C.E.
       Dawkins.]

145   *Athenaeum*, 2979(29 Nov 1884):692. [By (?-)
       Sergeant. Unsigned.]

146   *Graphic*, 30(27 Dec 1884):674.

147   *Saturday Review*, 59(27 June 1885):867-8.

148   *Spectator*, 57(13 Dec 1884):1666-7. [By
       Captain Clarke. Unsigned.]

A Stern Chase

149   *Academy*, 29(19 June 1886):430. [Signed
       Richard F. Littledale.]

150   *Athenaeum*, 3058(5 June 1886):745. [By (?-)
       Sergeant. Unsigned.]

151   *Graphic*, 34(31 July 1886):122.

152   *Saturday Review*, 62(28 Aug 1886):299.

153   *Spectator*, 59(26 June 1886):851-2. [By
       William Wallace. Unsigned.]

154   Allibone, S.A. See under Kirk, J.F.

155   *Author, The.* Par, 2(Jan 1892):248. [See
       INTRODUCTION.]

156   Bentley, Richard, and Son. *The Archives of
       Richard Bentley and Son.* British Library.
       Microfilm, Cambridge: Chadwyck-Healey,
       1976, Part 1, Reels 1,2,41,48. [Record of
       payments to, and copies of letters to,
       FCH. Report on her novel, *Chapter and
       Verse*; see above, INTRODUCTION.]

157   Chambers, W. and R. Manuscript papers, on
       temporary deposit in the National Library
       of Scotland. TD1709. [See also
       INTRODUCTION, and VI JOURNALISM (*Chambers's
       Journal*).]

158   *Dictionary of National Biography* ['E.L.': i.e.
       Elizabeth Lee]. Supplement 1901-1911,
       pp.276-7.

159   Downey, Edmund. *Twenty Years Ago; A Book of
       Anecdote Illustrating Literary Life in
       London.* London: Hurst and Blackett, 1905,
       Dedication and p.46. [See INTRODUCTION,
       above.]

160   Duffy, Sir Charles Gavan. *My Life in Two
       Hemispheres.* 2 vols. London: Fisher
       Unwin, 1898, vol. 2, p.367.

161   Edwards, P.D. 'The English Publication of
       His Natural Life', *Australian Literary
       Studies*, 10(Oct 1982):520-6.

162   Elliott, Brian. *Marcus Clarke.* Oxford:
       Clarendon Press, 1958, pp.165-6.

163   Escott, T.H.S. *England; Its People, Polity,
       and Pursuits.* 2 vols. London: Cassell,
       Petter, Galpin, [1879], vol. 2, p.404.

164   Escott, T.H.S. *Masters of English Journalism*. London: Fisher Unwin, 1911, p.261.

165   ────────. *Anthony Trollope; His Public Services, Private Friends, and Literary Originals*. London: John Lane, 1913, pp. 149-50.

166   ────────. *Great Victorians*. London: Fisher Unwin, 1916, p.347.

167   Furlong, Mary and Hyde, Douglas. *Irish Literature; Section I, Irish Authors and Their Writings in Ten Volumes*. N.Y.: P.F. Collier, 1904, vol. 4, pp.1578-87. [Includes extract from FCH's novel *A Golden Sorrow*.]

168   Furniss, Harry. *Some Victorian Women; Good, Bad, and Indifferent*. London: Bodley Head, 1923, p.9.

169   Hogan, Robert (et al.). *Dictionary of Irish Literature*. Westport, Conn.: Greenwood Press, 1979, pp.297-8.

170   Kirk, J.F. *A Supplement to Allibone's Critical Dictionary of English Literature and British and American Authors*. Philadelphia: J.B. Lipincott, 1891, vol. 2, pp.834-5.

171   Mitchell, Sally. 'Sentiment and Suffering; Women's Recreational Reading in the 1860s', *Victorian Studies*, 21(Autumn 1977):29-45.

172   Nicoll, W. Robertson. *James Macdonell, Journalist*. New ed. London: Hodder and Stoughton, 1900, p.267. [I am grateful to Professor Robert H. Tener for drawing my attention to this reference.]

173   Read, Charles A. and O'Connor, T.P. *The Cabinet of Irish Literature*. London: Blackie, 1882, vol. 4, pp.253-8. [Includes extract from FCH's short story *No Sign*.]

174   Shaw, George Bernard. *Collected Letters 1874-1897*, ed. Dan H. Laurence. London: Max Reinhardt, 1965, pp.7-8,21,209.

175   Tinsley, William. *Random Recollections of an Old Publisher*. 2 vols. London: Simpkin Marshall, etc., 1900, vol. 1, pp.137-43.

176   *Tinsley's Magazine*. Pars, 48(Feb 1892):263, and March 1892, 357.

177   W———, W.F. 'E.Y.', *Pall Mall Gazette*, 31 Oct 1900, p.1. [See INTRODUCTION, above.]

178   *Who Was Who*. 1897-1916, p.344.

ADDENDA AND CORRIGENDA

115A MANUSCRIPTS - University of Illinois Library.
8 ALS to the publisher and novelist Grant
Richards, 1905-8. *The Archives of Grant Richards,
1897-1948*. Microfilm, Cambridge: Chadwyck-
Healey, 1979, Reel 60. [See INTRODUCTION, p.31.
The Archives also contain letters from Richards
to FCH. (Reels 2, 9, and 11.)]

174A Swan Sonnenschein and Co. *The Archives of Swan
Sonnenschein and Co., 1878-1911*. Microfilm,
Bishops Stortford: Chadwyck-Healey, 1973,
Reel 17 (vol. 32, p.755).